OLD BEAR
DIARY

OLD BEAR
DIARY

EBURY PRESS STATIONERY

First published in 1991 by Ebury Press Stationery
An imprint of the Random Century Group
Random Century House, 20 Vauxhall Bridge Road,
London SW1V 2SA

Copyright © Random Century Group 1991
Illustrations copyright © Jane Hissey
Whilst every effort has been made to ensure accuracy, the publishers cannot accept
liability for errors.
All rights reserved. No part of this book may be reproduced in any form or by any
means without permission in writing from the publisher.

Set in Horley Old Style
by FMT Graphics Limited, Southwark, London
Printed and bound in Singapore
ISBN 0 7126 4519 5

This diary belongs to

Name

Address

December 1991 – January 1992

30 Monday Week 1

31 Tuesday

1 Wednesday

New Year's Day Holiday

2 Thursday

Bank Holiday, Scotland

3 Friday

January

4 Saturday •

5 Sunday

January

6 Monday　　　　　　　　　　　　　　　　　　　　　Week 2

Epiphany (Twelfth Night)

7 Tuesday

8 Wednesday

9 Thursday

10 Friday

January

11 Saturday

12 Sunday

JANUARY

13 Monday ☽   Week 3

14 Tuesday

15 Wednesday

16 Thursday

17 Friday

January

18 Saturday

19 Sunday ○

JANUARY

20 Monday Week 4

Holiday, USA (Martin Luther King's Birthday)

21 Tuesday

22 Wednesday

23 Thursday

24 Friday

January

25 Saturday

26 Sunday ◐

Australia Day

January – February

27 Monday   Week 5

Holiday, Australia (Australia Day)

28 Tuesday

29 Wednesday

30 Thursday

31 Friday

FEBRUARY

1 Saturday

2 Sunday

FEBRUARY

3 Monday ●   Week 6

4 Tuesday

5 Wednesday

6 Thursday

Holiday, NZ (Waitangi Day)

7 Friday

FEBRUARY

8 Saturday

9 Sunday

February

10 Monday Week 7

11 Tuesday ◐

12 Wednesday

13 Thursday

14 Friday

St Valentine's Day

February

15 Saturday

16 Sunday

February

17 Monday　　　　　　　　　　　　　　　　　　　　　　　Week 8

Holiday, USA (Washington's Birthday)

18 Tuesday　○

19 Wednesday

20 Thursday

21 Friday

FEBRUARY

22 Saturday

23 Sunday

February

24 Monday   Week 9

25 Tuesday ◐

26 Wednesday

27 Thursday

28 Friday

February – March

29 Saturday

1 Sunday

St David's Day, Wales

MARCH

2 Monday   Week 10

3 Tuesday

Shrove Tuesday

4 Wednesday   ●

Ash Wednesday

5 Thursday

Ramadan begins (subject to sighting of moon)

6 Friday

March

7 Saturday

8 Sunday

March

9 Monday
Week 11

Commonwealth Day

10 Tuesday

11 Wednesday

12 Thursday ☽

13 Friday

March

14 Saturday

15 Sunday

March

16 Monday   Week 12

17 Tuesday

St Patrick's Day, Ireland

18 Wednesday ○

19 Thursday

20 Friday

Vernal Equinox

MARCH

21 Saturday

22 Sunday

MARCH

23 Monday   Week 13

24 Tuesday

25 Wednesday

26 Thursday ☽

27 Friday

March

28 Saturday

29 Sunday

British Summer Time begins. Mother's Day, UK

March – April

30 Monday   Week 14

---

31 Tuesday

---

1 Wednesday

---

2 Thursday

---

3 Friday ●

APRIL

4 Saturday

5 Sunday

APRIL

6 Monday Week 15

Islamic Festival of Eid-ul-Fitre (subject to confirmation)

7 Tuesday

8 Wednesday

9 Thursday

10 Friday ☽

April

11 Saturday

12 Sunday

Palm Sunday

April

13 Monday   Week 16

14 Tuesday

15 Wednesday

16 Thursday

Maundy Thursday

17 Friday   ○

Good Friday Holiday

April

18 Saturday

Jewish Festival of Passover (Pesach) 1st day

19 Sunday

Easter Day

April

20 Monday   Week 17

Easter Monday Holiday (exc. Scotland and USA)

21 Tuesday

22 Wednesday

23 Thursday

St George's Day, England

24 Friday ☾

Jewish Festival of Passover (Pesach) 7th day

April

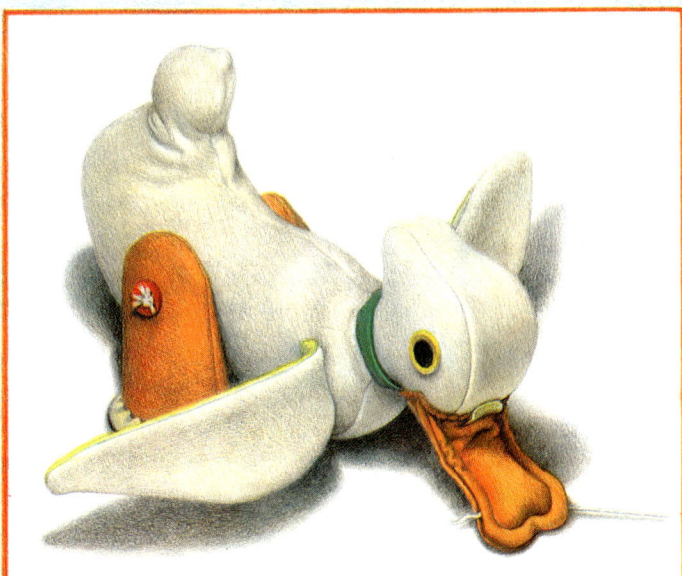

25 Saturday

Anzac Day, Australia, NZ

26 Sunday

April – May

27 Monday   Week 18

28 Tuesday

29 Wednesday

30 Thursday

1 Friday

May

2 Saturday ●

3 Sunday

May

4 Monday
Week 19

May Day Holiday, UK (exc. Scotland). Spring Holiday, Scotland

5 Tuesday

6 Wednesday

7 Thursday

8 Friday

May

9 Saturday ◐

10 Sunday

Mothering Sunday, USA

MAY

11 Monday　　　　　　　　　　　　　　　　　　　　　　　Week 20

12 Tuesday

13 Wednesday

14 Thursday

15 Friday

May

16 Saturday ○

17 Sunday

MAY

18 Monday
Week 21

Holiday, Canada (Victoria Day)

19 Tuesday

20 Wednesday

21 Thursday

22 Friday

MAY

23 Saturday

24 Sunday ◐

May

25 Monday   Week 22

May Day Holiday, Scotland, Spring Holiday, UK (exc. Scotland),
Memorial Day, USA

26 Tuesday

27 Wednesday

28 Thursday

Ascension Day

29 Friday

May

30 Saturday

31 Sunday

JUNE

1 Monday ●   Week 23

Holiday, NZ (Queen's Birthday)

2 Tuesday

3 Wednesday

4 Thursday

5 Friday

June

6 Saturday

7 Sunday ◐

Whit Sunday, Jewish Feast of Weeks (Shavuot)

JUNE

8 Monday   Week 24

9 Tuesday

10 Wednesday

11 Thursday

12 Friday

June

13 Saturday

14 Sunday

Trinity Sunday

June

15 Monday   ○   Week 25

---

16 Tuesday

---

17 Wednesday

---

18 Thursday

Corpus Christi

---

19 Friday

June

20 Saturday

21 Sunday

Summer Solstice. Father's Day, UK, USA

JUNE

22 Monday   Week 26

---

23 Tuesday ◐

---

24 Wednesday

---

25 Thursday

---

26 Friday

JUNE

27 Saturday

28 Sunday

June – July

29 Monday
Week 27

30 Tuesday ●

1 Wednesday

Holiday, Canada (Canada Day)

2 Thursday

Islamic New Year (subject to sighting of moon)

3 Friday

July

4 Saturday

Independence Day, USA

5 Sunday

July

6 Monday   Week 28

7 Tuesday ☽

8 Wednesday

9 Thursday

10 Friday

July

---

11 Saturday

---

12 Sunday

JULY

13 Monday
Week 29

Battle of the Boyne Holiday, N.Ireland
Islamic Festival of Eid-ul-Adha (subject to confirmation)

14 Tuesday ○

15 Wednesday

St Swithin's Day

16 Thursday

17 Friday

July

18 Saturday

19 Sunday

July

20 Monday   Week 30

21 Tuesday

22 Wednesday ☽

23 Thursday

24 Friday

JULY

25 Saturday

26 Sunday

July

27 Monday	Week 31

28 Tuesday

29 Wednesday ●

30 Thursday

31 Friday

August

1 Saturday

2 Sunday

August

3 Monday
Week 32

Summer Holiday, Scotland

4 Tuesday

5 Wednesday ◐

6 Thursday

7 Friday

August

8 Saturday

9 Sunday

August

10 Monday — Week 33

11 Tuesday

12 Wednesday

13 Thursday ○

14 Friday

August

15 Saturday

16 Sunday

AUGUST

17 Monday　　　　　　　　　　　　　　　　　　　　　　Week 34

18 Tuesday

19 Wednesday

20 Thursday

21 Friday ☽

AUGUST

22 Saturday

23 Sunday

August

24 Monday · Week 35

25 Tuesday

26 Wednesday

27 Thursday

28 Friday ●

August

29 Saturday

30 Sunday

August – September

31 Monday
Week 36

Summer Holiday, UK (exc. Scotland)

1 Tuesday

2 Wednesday

3 Thursday ☽

4 Friday

September

5 Saturday

6 Sunday

September

7 Monday

Week 37

Holiday, Canada (Labour Day), USA (Labor Day)

8 Tuesday

9 Wednesday

10 Thursday

11 Friday

September

12 Saturday   ○

13 Sunday

September

14 Monday · Week 38

15 Tuesday

16 Wednesday

17 Thursday

18 Friday

September

19 Saturday ◐

20 Sunday

September

21 Monday   Week 39

22 Tuesday

Autumnal Equinox

23 Wednesday

24 Thursday

25 Friday

September

26 Saturday •

27 Sunday

September – October

28 Monday Week 40

Jewish New Year (Rosh Hashanah)

29 Tuesday

30 Wednesday

1 Thursday

2 Friday

OCTOBER

3 Saturday ☽

4 Sunday

October

5 Monday   Week 41

6 Tuesday

7 Wednesday

Jewish Day of Atonement (Yom Kippur)

8 Thursday

9 Friday

OCTOBER

10 Saturday

11 Sunday ○

October

12 Monday   Week 42

Jewish Festival of Tabernacles (Succoth) 1st day. Holiday, Canada (Thanksgiving)
Holiday, USA (Columbus Day)

13 Tuesday

14 Wednesday

15 Thursday

16 Friday

OCTOBER

17 Saturday

18 Sunday

OCTOBER

19 Monday ◐
Week 43

Jewish Festival of Tabernacles (Succoth) 8th day

20 Tuesday

21 Wednesday

22 Thursday

23 Friday

OCTOBER

24 Saturday

United Nations' Day

25 Sunday ●

British Summer Time ends

OCTOBER

26 Monday　　　　　　　　　　　　　　　　　　　　　　　Week 44

Holiday, NZ (Labour Day)

27 Tuesday

28 Wednesday

29 Thursday

30 Friday

October – November

31 Saturday

Hallowe'en

1 Sunday

All Saints' Day

November

2 Monday ☽　　　　　　　　　　　　　　　　　　　Week 45

---

3 Tuesday

---

4 Wednesday

---

5 Thursday

Guy Fawkes' Day, UK

---

6 Friday

November

7 Saturday

8 Sunday

Remembrance Sunday

November

9 Monday   Week 46

10 Tuesday   ○

11 Wednesday

Holiday, USA (Armistice/Veterans' Day)
Holiday, Canada (Remembrance Day)

12 Thursday

13 Friday

NOVEMBER

14 Saturday

15 Sunday

November

16 Monday
Week 47

17 Tuesday ☽

18 Wednesday

19 Thursday

20 Friday

November

21 Saturday

22 Sunday

November

23 Monday   Week 48

24 Tuesday ●

25 Wednesday

26 Thursday

Holiday, USA (Thanksgiving Day)

27 Friday

November

28 Saturday

29 Sunday

Advent Sunday

November – December

30 Monday　　　　　　　　　　　　　　　　　　　　Week 49

St Andrew's Day, Scotland

1 Tuesday

2 Wednesday ☽

3 Thursday

4 Friday

December

5 Saturday

6 Sunday

DECEMBER

7 Monday   Week 50

8 Tuesday

9 Wednesday   ○

10 Thursday

11 Friday

DECEMBER

12 Saturday

13 Sunday

December

14 Monday   Week 51

15 Tuesday

16 Wednesday ☽

17 Thursday

18 Friday

December

19 Saturday

20 Sunday

December

21 Monday
Week 52

Winter Solstice

22 Tuesday

23 Wednesday

24 Thursday ●

Christmas Eve

25 Friday

Christmas Day Holiday

December

26 Saturday

Boxing Day

27 Sunday

December 1992 – January 1993

28 Monday

Holiday, UK (subject to confirmation)

29 Tuesday

30 Wednesday

31 Thursday

1 Friday

New Year's Day Holiday

JANUARY

2 Saturday

3 Sunday

JANUARY 1993

4 Monday

Bank holiday, Scotland (subject to confirmation)

5 Tuesday

6 Wednesday

7 Thursday

8 Friday